BUILT FOR SPEED
MOTORBIKES

IAN GRAHAM

Belitha Press

First published in the UK in 1998 by

Belitha Press Limited
London House, Great Eastern Wharf,
Parkgate Road, London SW11 4NQ

Copyright © in this format Belitha Press Ltd 1998
Text copyright © Ian Graham 1998
First published in paperback 1998

All rights reserved. No part of this book may be reproduced or utilized in any form or by any means, electronic or mechanical, including photocopying, recording or by any information storage and retrieval system, without permission in writing from the publisher except by a reviewer who may quote brief passages in a review.

ISBN 1 85561 710 2 (hardback)
ISBN 1 85561 830 3 (paperback)

British Library Cataloguing in Publication Data for this book is available from the British Library.

Printed in Hong Kong

Editor: Stephanie Bellwood
Designer: Dave Goodman
Series design: Helen James
Illustrator: Tom Connell
Picture researcher: Juliet Duff
Consultants: Craig Carey-Clinch, Motorcycle Action Group
Ann Robinson

Picture acknowledgements:
Action-Plus: 25 Keith Clarke. Allsport: 7 Anton Want, 13 bottom Mike Cooper, 15 Simon Bruty, 20 Anton Want, 21 Mike Cooper, 23 centre Agence Vandystadt, 23 bottom Mike Hewitt. Alvey and Towers: 18. BMW (GB) Ltd: 8, 10. Business Builders/Aprilia UK: 28 bottom. CHAM:11. Colorsport: 14 Sipa-Sport. Photographs courtesy of the Harley-Davidson Motor Company Archives: 19, 27 © H-D Michigan Inc. Honda UK: 6. Don Morley: 26. Quadrant Picture Library: 9, 16 top and bottom Gold and Goose © Roland Brown, 28 top Roland Brown, 29 top right Roland Brown. Rex Features: 13 centre Phil Masters, 24 © Sipa-Press, 29 top left.

Words in **bold** are explained in the glossary on pages 30 and 31.

Contents

The quest for speed	4
Designing for speed	6
On the drawing board	8
Will it work?	10
Engine power	12
Smooth riding	14
Tyre tracks	16
Superbikes	18
Track stars	20
Off-road racers	22
Drag racing	24
Record breakers	26
Shaping the future	28
Glossary	30
Index	32

The quest for speed

People are always trying to travel faster and faster. Designers are creating better, more powerful new bikes all the time. There are many types of motorbikes for all kinds of racing both on and off race tracks. Road bikes are based on new racing designs. This book shows how the best motorbikes are built for speed.

▲ Grand Prix racers
Grand Prix motorbikes are the stars of the world's racetracks. They twist and turn around motor racing **circuits** at speeds of more than 250 km/h.

▶ Drag bikes
Dragsters race like rockets down a straight track in a mad dash for the finish line.

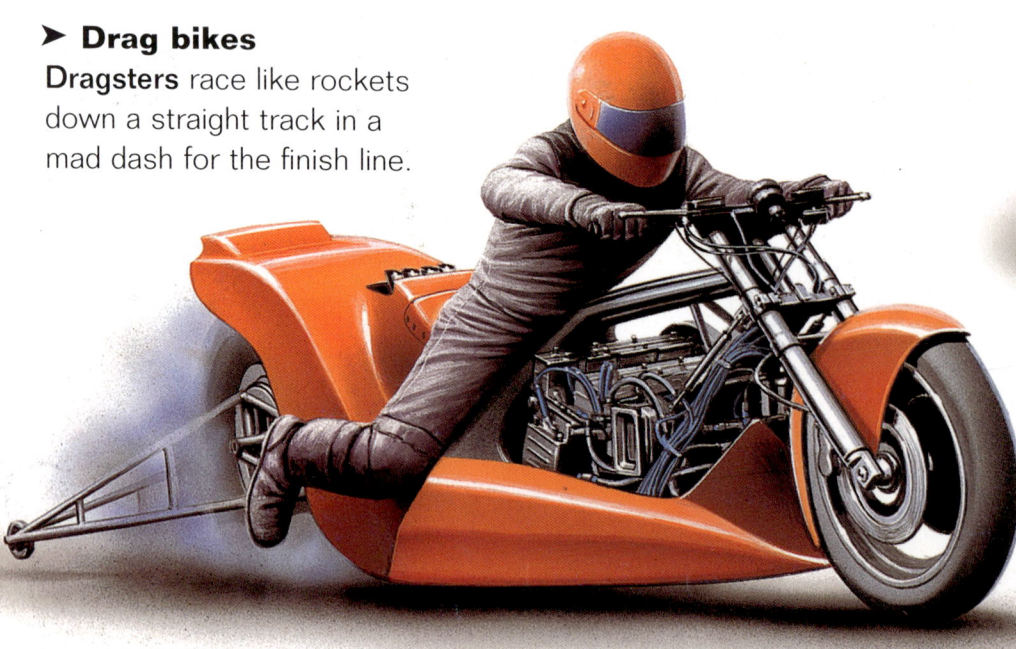

▼ **Speedy superbikes**
Superbikes are lightweight, **streamlined** speed machines. They are the fastest motorbikes built for riding on roads.

Kawasaki *ZX-9R*

▲ **Off-road riding**
Speedway riders skid and slide around rough dirt tracks. Their specially-designed bikes have no **gears** or brakes.

▼ **Amazing machines**
The fastest motorbikes of all are the bullet-shaped vehicles built to set world speed records.

Designing for speed

The performance of a motorbike depends on power, weight and shape. A specially-developed engine gives the bike its power. These engines are very heavy, so designers make sure that the frame of the bike is made from light but strong materials. It is also important that the motorbike is designed to be as **streamlined** as possible.

▼ Fast and fiery
The top-selling Honda *Fireblade* has a powerful engine and a lightweight frame which makes it fast and easy to ride. Its top speed is 265 km/h.

◄ High-tech headlights
The large headlight on the front of a motorbike spoils its streamlined shape. The Honda *Super Blackbird* superbike has a thinner, pointed headlight that gives the nose of the bike a much smoother shape.

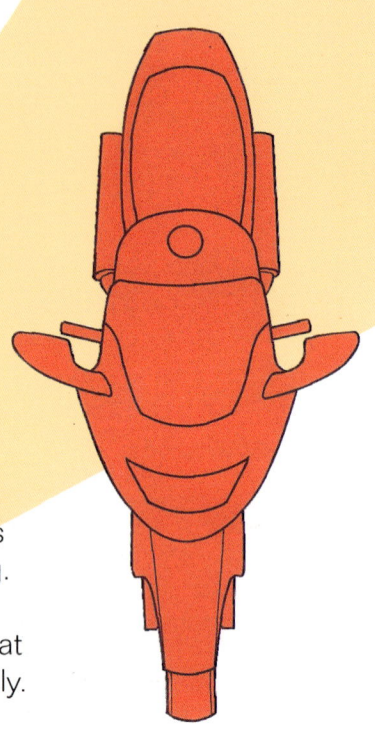

► Shaping the bike
Air pushes against a vehicle as it travels at speed. This is called air resistance, or **drag**. Motorbikes are designed to be smooth and curved so that they slip through the air easily.

▲ The motorbike rider
A motorbike is the only vehicle in which the rider sits on the outside and forms part of the overall shape. Designers have to think about the position of the rider when they are planning a new motorbike model.

Honda *Fireblade*

FAST FACTS
An engine needs to take in air to burn fuel. This means that the motorbike **fairing** must have holes in it for air to enter. Some of the air rushing past the moving bike is **channelled** through the holes and into the engine.

▶ Improving the design
Early motorbikes had an awkward, upright shape that created a lot of drag. Modern sports and racing motorbikes have a streamlined shape and a lower riding position so that air flows smoothly around the bike without slowing it down.

On the drawing board

Designers of modern motorbikes use computer-aided design systems to create amazing new vehicles. Every part of a motorbike can be drawn on computer. The designer turns the images around on screen and makes changes easily without having to re-draw plans by hand.

▲ Creating a new design
Before the designer makes any plans on computer, he or she needs to have an idea of how the design will look. Designers make detailed **sketches** on paper. They model the computer design on these drawings.

FAST FACTS
Some designers are working on ways of making riding at night much safer. One idea is to have a camera on the rider's helmet that displays a clear, bright image of dark roads ahead.

Types of chassis
The **chassis** is the basic frame of the motorbike. It has to be very strong to carry the weight of the motorbike and to cope with travelling at high speeds.

Most modern bikes have a **twin spar chassis**. Motorbikes made by the Italian Ducati company have a different type of chassis. It is a ladder-like frame of metal tubes called a **tubular steel chassis**.

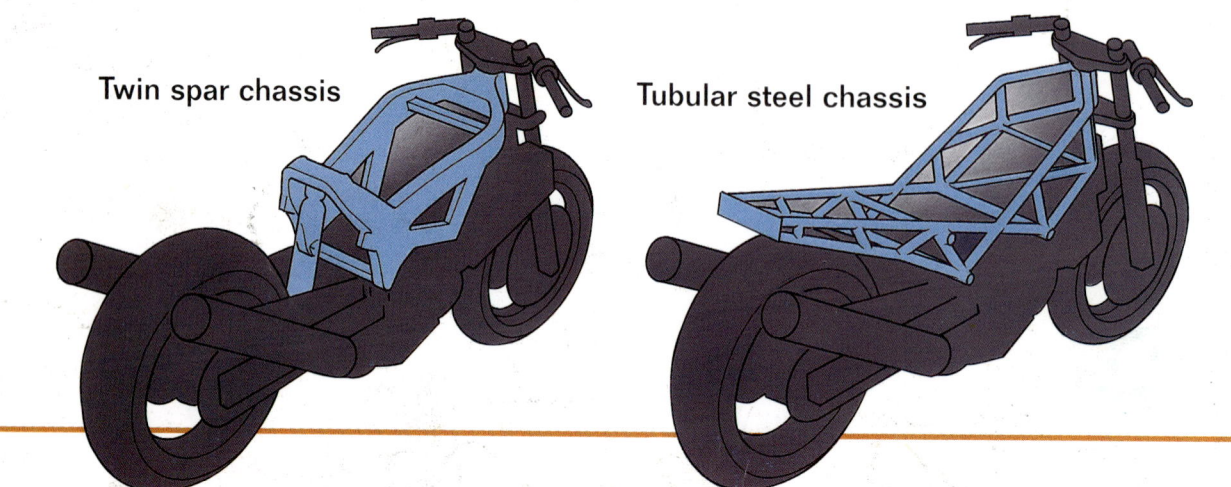

Twin spar chassis

Tubular steel chassis

engine temperature **gauge**

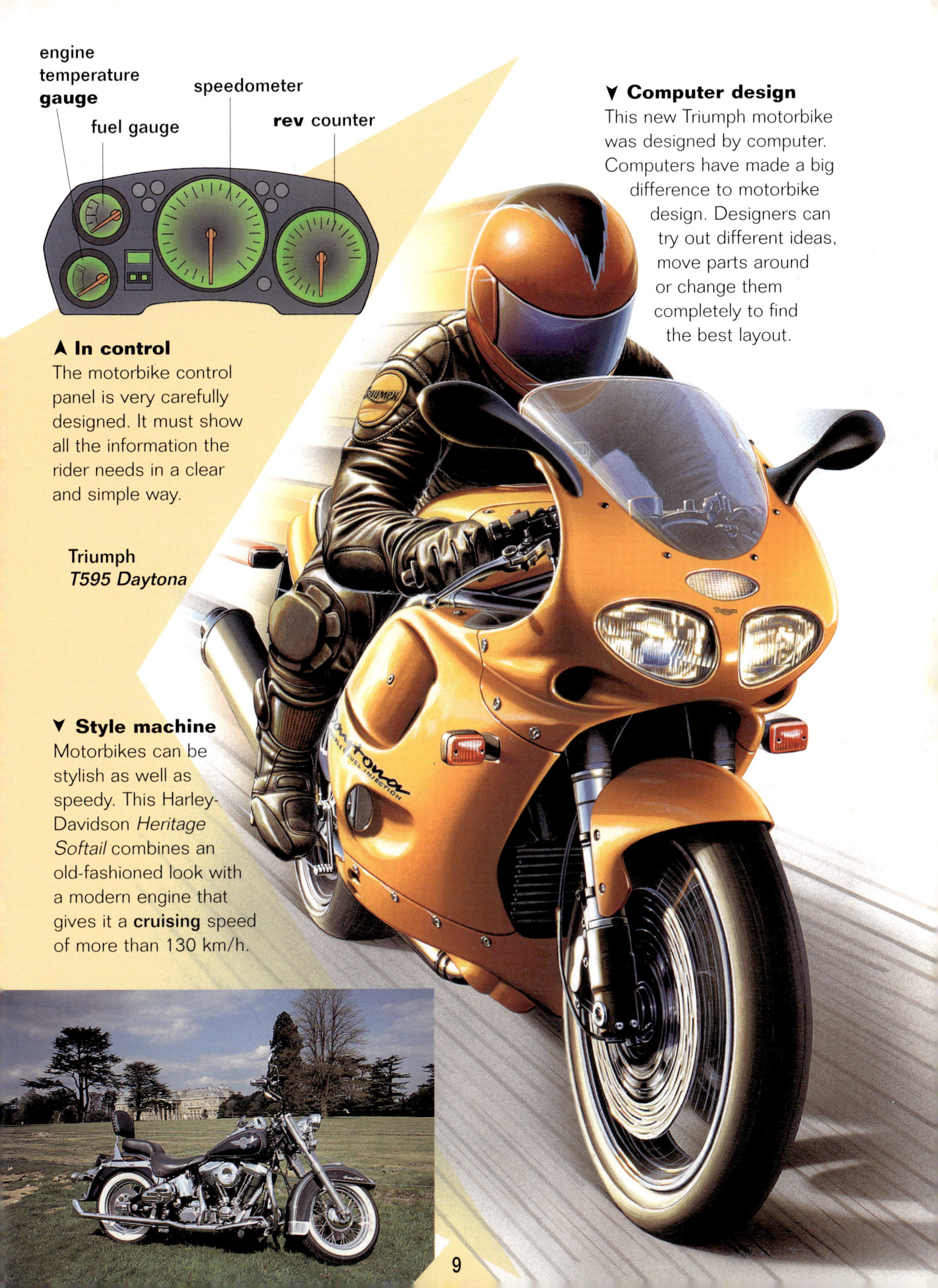

fuel gauge

speedometer

rev counter

▲ In control
The motorbike control panel is very carefully designed. It must show all the information the rider needs in a clear and simple way.

Triumph *T595 Daytona*

▼ Style machine
Motorbikes can be stylish as well as speedy. This Harley-Davidson *Heritage Softail* combines an old-fashioned look with a modern engine that gives it a **cruising** speed of more than 130 km/h.

▼ Computer design
This new Triumph motorbike was designed by computer. Computers have made a big difference to motorbike design. Designers can try out different ideas, move parts around or change them completely to find the best layout.

Will it work?

A new motorbike must be tested carefully before it is ready to be sold or raced. Computers check that it is the right shape and weight so that it will not become unsafe at high speeds. The finished design is checked by testing a model in a **wind tunnel**. Finally a **prototype** is built.

▼ **In the wind tunnel**
A motorbike model is placed in a wind tunnel. A rider sits on the model to check that air flows smoothly around the bike. The air flow can be seen by adding coloured smoke.

Honda model in a wind tunnel

◄ **Covered in paint**
In some wind tunnel tests the air is mixed with a special paint that sprays over the motorbike and the rider. This makes the air flow round the bike and rider easy to see.

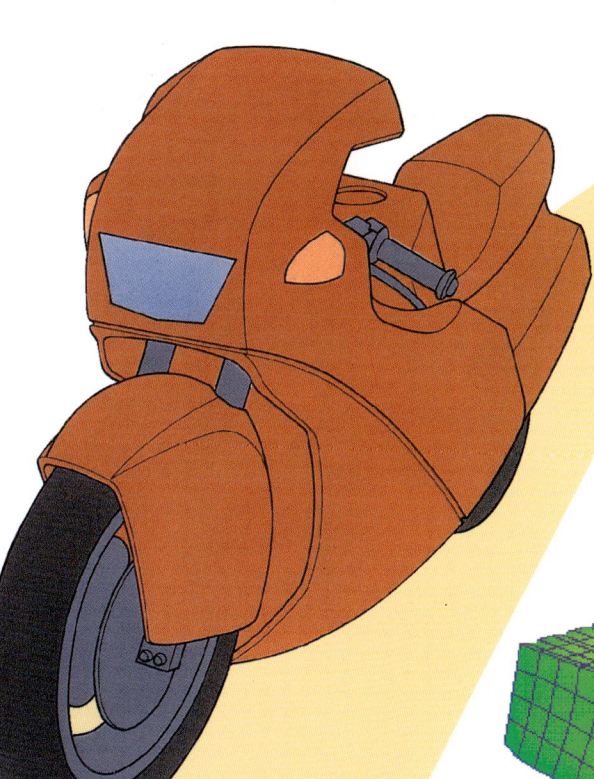

◀ Making models
Models of the new motorbike are made using clay to shape the **fairing**. Designers can then check that the whole body of the bike is smooth and **streamlined**.

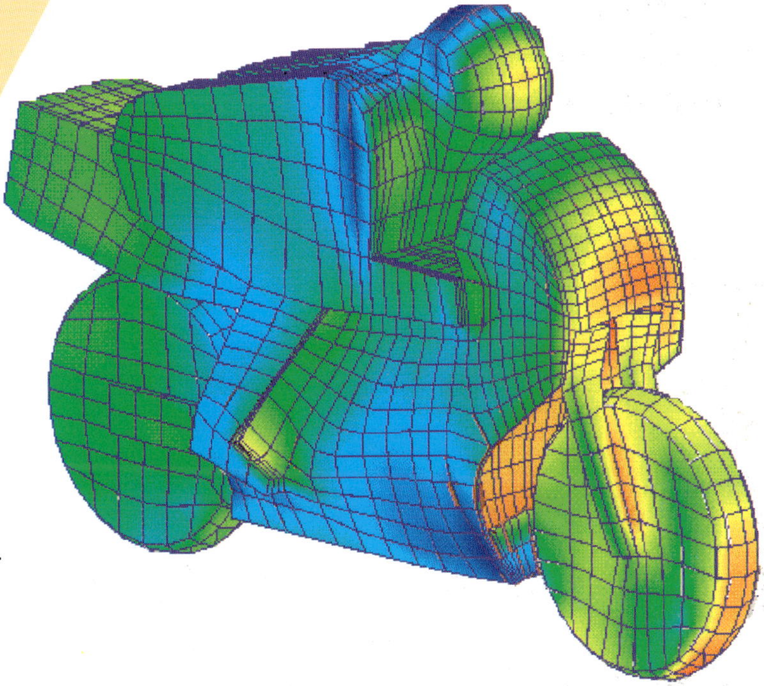

▶ Under pressure
This computer **simulation** is coloured to show where air will push most against the rider and the motorbike. The lighter parts will have to be the strongest.

▶ Safer riding
Motorbikes could soon have **air bags** just like cars. The air bag is folded inside the crash helmet and it inflates automatically if the rider is thrown off the bike. The air bag keeps the rider's head upright to prevent neck injuries.

air bag

FAST FACTS
Racing motorbikes are always being updated and changed. Designers have to be very careful when they alter the design of a bike. It is vital that nothing goes wrong when the bike is racing along at speeds of around 300 km/h.

Engine power

Many of the fastest motorbikes in the world are powered by **piston engines** just like ordinary family cars. But the engines of sports and racing bikes are much more highly developed. Sometimes they burn a special fuel instead of petrol to help the bike to reach even higher speeds.

Kawasaki *ZZ-R1000*

Extra power

Some fast motorbikes carry a small container of gas called **nitrous oxide**. This gas can be sprayed into the engine where it burns and produces extra power. This gives the motorbike a quick explosive burst of speed.

▲ **Speed machine**
The Japanese Kawasaki *ZZ-R1000* was the fastest **production motorbike** in the world when it was launched in 1990. It has a top speed of 280 km/h.

➤ Muscle bike
Some motorbikes have an enormous, heavy engine that makes the whole bike look huge. These bikes are often called muscle bikes.

▲ Jet bikes
A few specially-built motorbikes use **jet engines**. Jet engines can be very dangerous. The bike is so powerful that it is difficult for the rider to control it without being thrown off.

◀ Pulling a wheelie
Some motorbikes have such powerful engines that the front wheel lifts off the ground as the bike moves fast. This is called pulling a wheelie.

Smooth riding

The wheels of a motorbike must be touching the ground at all times for the rider to be able to control the bike at speed. This means that the wheels have to follow every bump and hollow in the road. Motorbikes are fitted with springs called a **suspension** system. This lets the wheels bounce over rough surfaces while the main body of the motorbike moves along smoothly.

◀ **Suspension units**
A suspension unit is a spring that is wrapped around an oil-filled tube called a damper. Inside the damper is a **piston**. When the wheel hits a bump, the spring is squeezed down. It tries to bounce back but it is slowed down because the piston moves slowly through the thick oil.

spring

piston

oil-filled damper

◀ **On the road**
Motorbikes ride on all kinds of surfaces, so they need reliable suspension. This Yamaha bike is in a long-distance race from Paris in France to Dakar in Africa. The race covers all kinds of **terrain** including the desert.

Types of suspension

Most ordinary motorbikes have a suspension unit on each side of the rear wheel. It is a simple layout that works well for ordinary road bikes. Sports bikes have just one suspension unit near the middle of the bike. This lets the back wheel move around more.

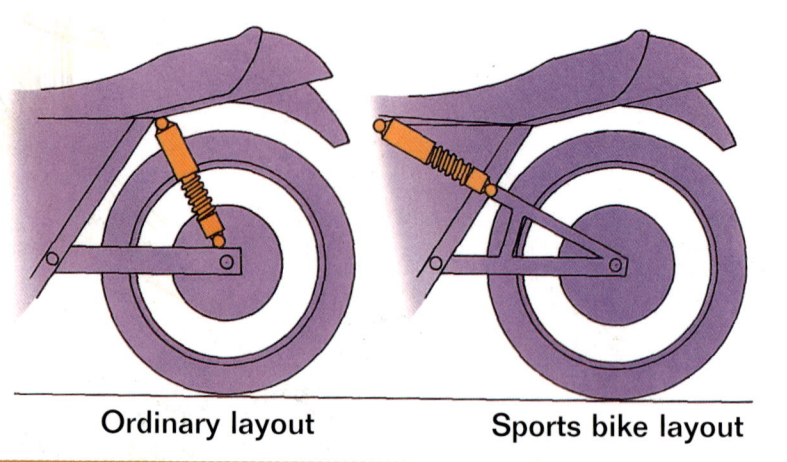

Ordinary layout   Sports bike layout

▲ Quick change
Racing motorbikes often have a suspension unit near the middle of the bike so that the wheels can be removed and replaced easily. This is very important when racing team mechanics need to work fast.

A motocross bike

▲ Difficult ground
Good suspension is vital for racing motorbikes that travel at high speed over rough terrain. Off-road bikes race in all kinds of weather on dirt tracks and rocky, hilly ground.

Tyre tracks

The job of a motorbike's tyres is to keep the bike firmly on the ground. Tyres are made from a special type of rubber that grips surfaces instead of sliding across them. Racing tyres are made from soft rubber that turns sticky when it warms up during a race. This gives the bike extra grip.

▲ Spinning wheels
Before a drag race, a drag bike's wheels are spun at high speed. The tyres heat up and become soft and sticky. This improves their grip and gives the bike a faster start.

▲ Round tyres
Motorbike tyres are more rounded than car tyres. This is because a motorbike leans over as it corners. It needs to keep the same area of rubber on the ground to stay in control.

FAST FACTS
The first motorbike, built in 1885, had wooden wheels. Most early motorbikes had solid rubber tyres. In 1888 air-filled, or pneumatic, tyres were invented to make motorbike riding much smoother.

▼ Tyre design
Motorbike tyres have to be hard-wearing. A tyre is made from a thick mixture of **steel**, rubber, plastics and fabric. It is kept in shape with tough bands of fabric that are called plies.

16

Slick tyre slides on wet surface

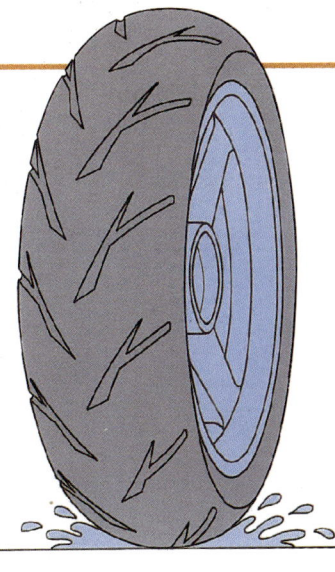

Wet weather tyre grips wet surface

Racing tyres

Tyres used for racing on dry tracks are smooth, or **slick**. They cannot be used in wet weather because water builds up underneath the tyre. This can cause the motorbike to spin out of control. Special wet weather tyres have a deep pattern of grooves called **tread** that let water run out from underneath the tyres. The bike then stays firmly on the ground.

▶ **Staying in control**
Racing tyres are often fatter than ordinary tyres. The wider the tyre is, the more rubber is on the track. This means that the bike has a better grip.

Superbikes

Superbikes are the fastest, most powerful and most expensive bikes on the road. Most of them are high performance machines, but slower bikes such as Harley-Davidsons and BMWs are also called superbikes because they are very stylish and popular. The fastest superbikes reach speeds of more than 250 km/h.

Ducati *916*

▼ **Fast and furious**
Superbike racing is becoming more and more popular. This is partly because riders use road bikes that have been **modified**. Superbike fans can buy ordinary versions of the bikes they see racing on the track.

◀ Harley-Davidson *VR1000*
The Harley-Davidson company is famous for producing bikes with an old-fashioned look, but they also created the *VR1000* superbike. It is designed to compete with the best Japanese and Italian racing bikes.

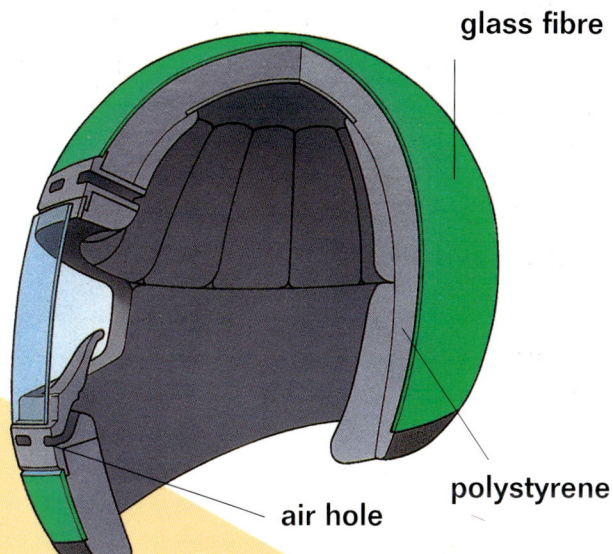

glass fibre

polystyrene

air hole

▲ Head protection
Motorbike riders must always wear a crash helmet. Helmets are made from **glass fibre**. The rider's head is cushioned by a thick layer of **polystyrene**. Tiny holes let air in to keep the rider's head cool.

◀ Red devil
The Ducati *916* is one of the most famous and distinctive superbikes in the world. Its highly-developed engine gives it a top speed of 257 km/h.

▶ Biking gear
Many superbike riders wear multi-coloured helmets, boots and one-piece suits called leathers. Leather is a very practical material to wear as it doesn't tear if it scrapes the ground.

Track stars

Grand Prix motorbike race

There are three main kinds of motorbike races held on race tracks. They are called Grand Prix, superbike and **endurance**. The fastest racers are Grand Prix bikes. They reach speeds of more than 320 km/h on the **straight**. Superbikes look like ordinary road bikes, but their engines are specially developed to produce much more power. Endurance races are long-distance events that last up to 24 hours.

▼ Keeping cool
Engines heat up while they are running. It is important that they do not overheat. Carefully-shaped holes in the bike's **fairing** let air flow around the engine. This stops it from becoming too hot.

◄ Hanging off the bike
Motorbikes lean towards the inside of a bend to stay balanced. Racing bikes turn corners so fast that the rider has to hang off the side to keep the bike in control. Riders lean over so far that their knee scrapes the ground.

FAST FACTS
Coloured flags are waved to give important messages as racing bikes flash past. A yellow flag warns of danger ahead, and a red flag tells the riders that the race has been stopped. The **chequered flag** marks the end of the race.

▶ Clever racing
A racing motorbike often follows closely behind another bike then pops out and overtakes on a bend. This trick is called **slipstreaming**. The leading bike has to battle against **drag** while the chasing bike has an easy ride.

▲ Championship racers
There are different types of Grand Prix bikes. The most advanced bikes race in the 500cc Grand Prix championship. Every Grand Prix motorbike is built by hand just like Formula One racing cars.

▲ Bikes built for two
Sidecar racing is an unusual-looking but popular motor sport. Motorbikes with sidecars do not lean into corners like ordinary bikes. Instead the passenger in the sidecar leans towards the inside of the track as the bike speeds round a corner.

Off-road racers

Motorbikes race on all sorts of surfaces. **Speedway** races are held on dirt tracks and sometimes on ice. **Motocross** racing is a cross-country event on muddy, hilly courses. **Supercross** racing is similar to motocross but it is held indoors on specially-built tracks. Each off-road event needs a different type of motorbike.

◀ **Super grip**
Motorbikes that climb hills need extra grip. The back wheel of the bike is often wrapped in chains or fitted with tyres that have spikes or cups.

▼ **Bikes without brakes**
Speedway is very dangerous because the bikes have no **gears** or brakes. As the bike slides round a corner, riders have to slam down one foot to stay upright.

Speedway bikes

FAST FACTS
American **hill-climbing** is an event in which bikes try to reach the top of very steep hills as quickly as possible. It is so difficult that sometimes no-one manages to reach the top of the hill. If this happens, the rider who climbed the furthest before dropping out is the winner.

▶ Double the fun
Sidecar motocross is one of the toughest motorbike sports events. The passenger has to hold on very tightly to avoid being thrown out on to the bumpy course.

Ice bikes
Ice racing is popular in parts of America, Scandinavia and Europe. Ice racing bikes have tyres covered with hundreds of long spikes so that they can grip the slippery surface of the track. A guard around the wheel protects the rider from the sharp spikes.

◀ Motocross racing
Motocross bikes are tall and have good **suspension** to help them cope with the uneven course. The tyres are knobbly to grip the loose dirt or mud surface. Riders fall off their motorbikes so often that they wear **body armour**, extra thick jeans and a strong helmet.

Drag racing

The aim of drag racing is to **accelerate** as fast as possible down a straight track called a drag strip. **Dragsters** are divided into classes and they race against each other in pairs. They have extremely powerful engines and often use special fuels instead of petrol. The fastest drag bikes travel at more than 300 km/h.

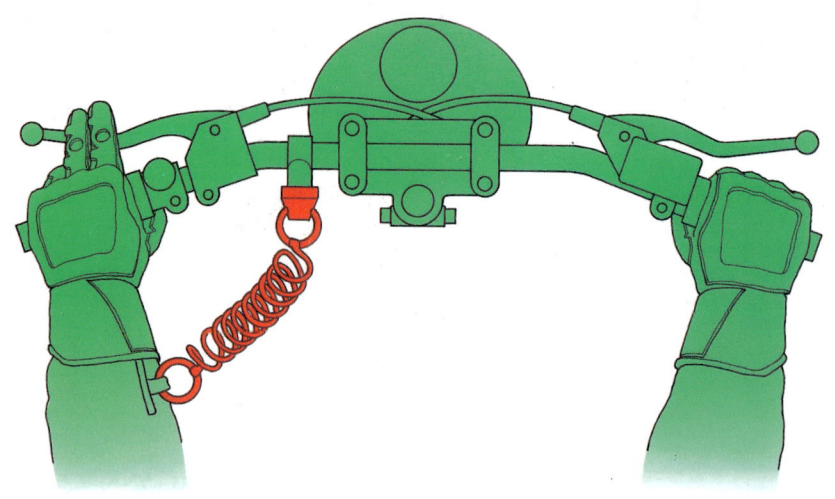

▲ **The kill switch**
If the rider falls off the motorbike during a race, it is important to stop the bike at once. A cable fixed to the rider's wrist is attached to an engine 'kill switch' on the handlebars. If the rider falls, the cable pulls the switch and turns the engine off.

▶ **Crazy racers**
A drag race is a thrilling sight but it is all over very quickly. Bikes race down the 402-metre drag strip in about seven seconds.

▼ **Dangerous driving**
Drag racing motorbikes are built to be as fast and powerful as possible. Some bikes even use the same type of **jet engine** that is usually used to power huge helicopters.

◀ **Riding position**
The shape of the bike is vital in a sport as fast as drag racing. Drag riders lie low over the front of the bike so that they are as **streamlined** as possible. Their weight helps to keep the front of the bike on the ground.

A drag bike

▲ **Wheelie bar**
A drag bike's engine is so powerful that it could make the bike pull a huge wheelie and flip over backwards. To stop this happening, a long bar with tiny wheels called a wheelie bar is fitted to the back of the bike.

Record breakers

Record breaking bikes look like long thin tubes. They are built in this way to be as **streamlined** as possible. The current world motorbike speed record is 518.45 km/h. It was set on July 14, 1990, by Dave Campos in a slim, metal machine called *Easyriders*. The bike was powered by two large Harley-Davidson engines.

▼ **Hidden motorbike**
The shape of a record-breaking bike is very important. The rider and the bike are enclosed inside a smooth, lightweight shell. The bike can then slip through the air easily.

FAST FACTS
The Bonneville Salt Flats International Speedway in Utah, USA, is one of the few places in the world with a track long, smooth and firm enough for motorbikes to **accelerate** to speeds of more than 500 km/h. It is a straight, narrow track more than 14 kilometres long.

◀ Trying to stop

When a motorbike sets a record it is moving so fast that brakes are not enough to stop it. It has to use a parachute to slow down.

◀ Changing shape

Early record-breaking bikes were just like ordinary motorbikes. This American bike broke the record in 1953. Its **fairing** is streamlined but the rider still sits on the outside of the bike.

▲ Uncomfortable riding

Cal Rayborn was a Harley-Davidson race rider. In 1970 he set a land speed record of 427 km/h in this machine. It was so low that he had to lie on his back to fit inside.

Lightning Bolt

▲ Lightning speed

Motorbike speed records are so high now that it is difficult to set a new record. The current record is only just faster than the last one of 512.733 km/h. This speed was set in 1978 by Don Vesco in *Lightning Bolt*. It was powered by two enormous Kawasaki engines.

Shaping the future

Motorbike companies are always trying to imagine how motorbikes might look in the future. One way of doing this is to design and build **concept** bikes. These are special experimental bikes that help designers to see how new technology can be used to create better, faster bikes. Who knows what kinds of amazing machines we may see on the roads and race tracks of the future?

▲ **City riding**
Some new bikes are designed to be practical for riding on busy roads. The engine is still powerful but the bike is as light and small as possible. This motorbike is called *Ultralite*.

▶ **Spectacular superbike**
This new Australian superbike **prototype** has a strong, extra-**streamlined** body and a huge engine. The bike will be able to travel faster than some sports cars.

▲ **Daring designs**
The Aprilia motorbike company is famous for stylish and successful sports bikes and **speedy** road bikes. This new concept motorbike is a good example of Aprilia's striking design style.

▲ **Riding on air**
The *Apache Warrior* is a futuristic **production motorbike** based on a concept bike. It has a new type of **suspension**. Instead of springs, it uses air cushions to absorb shocks.

▲ **Metallic machine**
Fashion is important to designers as they plan a new model. The designer of this unusual Harley motorbike used big, bold shapes and a metallic body to give the bike a special look.

Hunwick Hallum superbike

Glossary

accelerate
To move faster and faster.

air bag
A strong bag folded inside the helmet of a motorbike rider. In a crash, the air bag fills with gas to cushion the rider's neck. As soon as the crash is over, the gas escapes from the bag. Air bags are already used in cars, but the motorbike air bag is still being designed and developed.

body armour
A tough plastic vest worn by motocross riders to protect them from injuries.

channel
To make something go in a certain direction. Air is channelled into a motorbike engine through specially-shaped holes in the fairing.

chassis
The main motorbike frame. The rest of the motorbike is built up around this frame. The chassis has to be strong enough to support the weight of the whole bike.

chequered flag
A black and white checked flag used in motor racing. The chequered flag is waved to the winner and all the finishers in a race to tell them that the race is over.

circuit
A race route or course that is usually curved or circular.

concept
An idea. A concept bike is a designer's plan for a new motorbike. Designers create all kinds of amazing concept bikes. Some experimental motorbikes are made into production motorbikes later.

cruise
To travel at a steady speed. A vehicle's cruising speed is lower than its top speed.

drag
Drag, or air resistance, is the force that pushes against a motorbike or any other vehicle as it moves along. This slows the vehicle down. The faster the vehicle goes, the more drag there is. This is why the fastest motorbikes are extra-streamlined.

dragster
Dragsters are huge, powerful motorbikes that race down special tracks called drag strips. Dragsters are built by hand, so each one is different. Another name for a dragster is a drag bike.

endurance racing
Endurance means putting up with something difficult for a long time. Endurance races take place on tracks. They last for a set time that is sometimes as long as 24 hours. The winner is the rider or the team that covers the greatest distance in that time.

fairing
The outer covering of a motorbike. The fairing covers the engine and other workings of the motorbike. This makes the bike more streamlined.

gauge
Equipment for measuring something such as speed, temperature or fuel.

gears
The parts of a motorbike that change the bike's speed.

glass fibre
A strong, lightweight material used to cover surfaces that need to be strong, such as motorbike crash helmets.

hill-climbing
A type of motorbike sport. The motorbikes used in hill-climbing need to have a good grip so that they can power up steep hills. In Europe, hill-climbs take place on ordinary roads, but American hill-climbs are held on dirt tracks.

jet engine
A very powerful engine that is usually used by fast aircraft.

modify
To change or alter something to improve it.

motocross
An outdoor motorbike race across rough ground. There is also a type of motocross racing for cars.

nitrous oxide
A colourless gas that is used to boost the engine power of a motorbike.

piston
A metal disc that slides up and down in a hollow tube called a cylinder. Pistons are used to help to move or power something.

piston engine
The kind of engine that is used in most motorbikes and cars. Pistons are pushed up and down in cylinders to produce energy. The more cylinders the engine has, the more powerful it is.

polystyrene
A light but firm material used for padding and packing.

production motorbike
A motorbike that is one of many identical motorbikes made in a factory and sold to the public.

prototype
The first full-size motorbike that is built using a new design. The prototype is tested to make sure that it works properly. Then more bikes are made and sold.

rev
The word rev is short for revolution. A revolution is one full turn of a part of the motorbike engine called the shaft. The engine speed is often measured by how many revs it makes every minute.

simulation
A computer image of a new design that shows what a motorbike will be like when it is built. Designers study computer simulations of a motorbike to see if there are any problems and to think of ways to improve the design.

sketch
A rough drawing. Motorbike designers make sketches of their ideas before they begin to work on computer.

slick
The name for a smooth racing tyre. Motorbikes are fitted with slick tyres when they are racing in dry weather.

slipstreaming
A trick used in motor racing. One motorbike follows closely behind another motorbike. It does this to shelter from the oncoming wind and to avoid being slowed down by air resistance, or drag. Racing cars also use this method.

speedway
An off-road motorbike sport. Riders race on lightweight, powerful motorbikes around an oval dirt track. Speedway motorbikes sometimes use special fuels instead of petrol. This means that they can hurtle round the track at dangerously high speeds.

steel
A type of metal. Steel is very strong and it can be shaped and moulded easily. It is a good material for making motorbike parts.

straight
A long, straight part of a race track. Racing bikes accelerate along the straight but they have to slow down at the corners or they would spin out of control.

streamlined
A smooth, slim shape. Fast motorbikes are designed to be as streamlined as possible so that they can slip through the air without being slowed down by drag. The rider has to lean forward so that he or she doesn't spoil the shape.

supercross
Supercross is an off-road racing event. It is very similar to motocross but it is held indoors. A special dirt track is built in a large sporting arena.

suspension
A motorbike's suspension is a system of springs. The springs support the motorbike and stop it from being jolted and shaken around when it rides over bumps and hollows in the road. This makes the journey more comfortable for the rider. It also makes the motorbike easier to control.

terrain
Another word for ground. The word terrain is often used to describe rough, hilly or dangerous ground that is difficult for bikes to ride on.

tread
The grooves in a rubber tyre. Tread helps the tyre to grip the road or track.

tubular steel chassis
A chassis made of thin metal tubes that are strong enough to support the bike's weight.

twin spar chassis
The most common type of chassis used for motorbikes. A twin spar chassis is made of strong metal moulded into a thick frame. It is wrapped around the engine.

wind tunnel
A tunnel with a strong wind blowing through it. A model motorbike is placed inside the wind tunnel. Designers watch the air flow to check that the motorbike is streamlined.

Index

accelerate 24, 26, 30
air bag 11, 30
air resistance 6
Apache Warrior 29
Aprilia 28

BMW 18
body armour 23, 30
Bonneville Salt Flats
    International Speedway 26
brakes 5, 22, 27

Campos, Dave 26
chained tyre 22
chassis 8, 30
chequered flag 21, 30
circuit 4, 30
computer design 8, 9, 10, 11
concept motorbike 28, 29, 30
control panel 9
cornering 16, 20, 22
crash helmet 8, 11, 19, 23
cruise 9, 30
cupped tyre 22

damper 14
desert riding 14
drag 6, 7, 21, 30
drag racing 16, 24, 25
dragster 4, 16, 24, 25, 30
drag strip 24
Ducati 8, 18, 19
Ducati *916* 18, 19

early motorbike 7, 16, 26, 27
Easyriders 26
endurance racing 20, 30
engine 6, 7, 9, 12, 13, 19, 20, 24, 25, 26, 27, 28
engine temperature gauge 9

fairing 7, 11, 20, 27, 30
frame 6, 8
fuel 7, 9, 12, 24
fuel gauge 9

gauge 9, 30
gears 5, 22, 30
glass fibre 19, 30
Grand Prix motorbike 4, 20, 21
grip 16, 17, 22

Harley-Davidson 9, 18, 19, 26, 27, 29
Harley-Davidson *Heritage Softail* 9
Harley-Davidson *VR1000* 19
headlight 6
hill-climbing 22, 30
Honda *Fireblade* 6, 7
Honda *Super Blackbird* 6, 10
Hunwick Hallum 28, 29

ice racing 22, 23
indoor racing 22

jet engine 13, 24, 30

Kawasaki 4, 5, 12, 13, 27
Kawasaki *ZX-9R* 4, 5
Kawasaki *ZZ-R1000* 12, 13
kill switch 24
knobbly tyre 23

leathers 19
Lightning Bolt 26, 27
long-distance race 14, 20

mechanic 15
motocross 15, 22, 23, 30
muscle bike 13

night riding 8
nitrous oxide 12, 30

off-road racing 5, 15, 22, 23
oil 14
overtaking 21

parachute 26, 27
piston 14, 30
piston engine 12, 31
plastic 16
pneumatic tyre 16
polystyrene 19, 31
production motorbike 12, 29, 31
prototype 10, 28, 31

racing motorbike 4, 7, 11, 12, 15, 16, 17, 18, 20, 21, 22, 23, 24, 25
Rayborn, Cal 27
record breaker 5, 26, 27
rev counter 9, 31
riding position 7, 25, 27
road bike 4, 5, 14, 18, 19, 20, 28, 29
rubber 16, 17

shape 6, 7, 10, 25, 26, 28, 29
sidecar racing 21, 23
sketch 8, 31
slick tyre 17, 31
slipstreaming 21, 31
speedometer 9
speed record 5, 26, 27
speedway 5, 22, 23, 31
spiked tyre 22, 23
sports motorbike 7, 12, 14, 28
spring 14, 29
steel 8, 16, 31
streamlining 5, 6, 7, 11, 25, 26, 27, 28, 31
superbike 5, 6, 18, 19, 20, 28, 29
supercross 22, 31
suspension 14, 15, 23, 29, 31
Suzuki 17

testing 10, 11
tread 17, 31
Triumph *T595 Daytona* 9
tubular steel chassis 8, 31
twin spar chassis 8, 31
tyre 16, 17, 22, 23

Ultralite 28

Vesco, Don 27

weight 6, 8, 10, 25, 28
wet weather tyre 17
wheel 13, 14, 15, 16, 22, 23
wheelie 13, 25
wheelie bar 25
wind tunnel 10, 31

Yamaha 14